The Carpetbaggers

by Lucia Raatma

Content Adviser: Dr. Paul Christopher Anderson, Associate Professor,
Department of History, Clemson University

Reading Adviser: Rosemary G. Palmer, Ph.D., Department of Literacy,
College of Education, Boise State University

COMPASS POINT BOOKS
MINNEAPOLIS, MINNESOTA

Compass Point Books
3109 West 50th Street, #115
Minneapolis, MN 55410

Visit Compass Point Books on the Internet at *www.compasspointbooks.com*
or e-mail your request to *custserv@compasspointbooks.com*

On the cover: A Northern carpetbagger talks with Southerners about new voting privileges.

Photographs ©: Bettmann/Corbis, cover, 8, 16, 19, 26, 39; MPI/Getty Images, 4, 35; Library of Congress, 5, 10, 24, 31, 32, 34, 36, 37; North Wind Picture Archives, 7, 11, 30, 33, 38; Stock Montage/Getty Images, 12; Corbis, 13, 40, 41; Stock Montage, 15; Library of Congress/Getty Images, 20; Collection of the Museum of Florida History, Florida Department of State, 21; Courtesy of South Caroliniana Library, University of South Carolina, Columbia, 23; Kean Collection/Getty Images, 25, 28; Texas State Library & Archives Commission, 29.

Creative Director: Terri Foley
Managing Editor: Catherine Neitge
Editor: Jennifer VanVoorst
Photo Researcher: Svetlana Zhurkina
Designer/Page production: Bradfordesign, Inc./Les Tranby
Cartographer: XNR Productions, Inc.
Educational Consultant: Diane Smolinski

Library of Congress Cataloging-in-Publication Data
Raatma, Lucia.
  The carpetbaggers / By Lucia Raatma.
    p. cm.— (We the people)
  Includes bibliographical references and index.
  ISBN 0-7565-0834-7
  1. Reconstruction (U.S. history, 1865-1877)—Juvenile literature. I. Title. II. We the
  people (Series) (Compass Point Books)
E668.R125 2005
975'.041—dc22   2004016342

TABLE OF CONTENTS

AFTER THE CIVIL WAR

Have you ever had a fight with someone and then had trouble making up after the disagreement was over? That's what the United States was faced with after the Civil War ended in April 1865. After four years of fighting, the Union, made up of Northern states, defeated the

Southern states that had withdrawn to form the Confederate States of America. After their victory, the people of the Northern states were eager to make the country whole again.

President Hayes and others attempted to reunite the North and the South after the Civil War.

4

The railroad depot in Richmond, Virginia, was destroyed during the Civil War.

However, many people in the Southern states were angry or in need of help. During the Civil War, property in the South had been burned or damaged. Southern cities that were once beautiful lay in ruin. A person from Virginia described it this way: "We had no cattle, hogs, sheep, horses or anything else. The barns were all burned, chimneys standing without houses and houses standing without roofs, or doors, or windows."

In addition to the physical destruction, there was no longer a functioning local government. There were no post offices and no police officers to keep the peace. It was time to rebuild.

While some Southerners were ready to rebuild their communities, others did not want to cooperate. They did not like the fact that former slaves were now free. They disapproved of the rights the African-Americans now had, and they did not want anyone from the North telling them what to do. Many Southern women, like those in the North, had lost their husbands in the war, so now they had to raise families by themselves. Many men who had survived the war had injuries to deal with. Some had lost arms or legs, and others suffered from wounded pride. They did not want to accept the defeat the North had handed them.

The 4 million newly freed slaves faced a different problem. Most had nowhere to live and no way to make a living. Since they had never been paid for their work, they had no money saved up. They were finally free, but they had few options.

In an effort to help these former slaves, Congress created the Freedmen's Bureau. This organization distributed clothing and food to both African-Americans and white Americans.

Members of the Freedmen's Bureau in Memphis discuss new laws.

The bureau also opened schools and tried to educate African-Americans. In the past, it had been illegal for slaves to learn to read or write. Now free, they were hungry for knowledge.

The Freedmen's Bureau opened schools to teach the former slaves how to read and write.

8

BEGINNING RECONSTRUCTION

Reconstruction is the name of the period after the Civil War when Americans tried to rebuild the South and the governments of Southern states. Many Southerners, however, also needed to rebuild their own view of the South. Although the end of the Civil War brought many changes to the South, a number of Southern leaders continued to think just as they had before the war. They felt that African-Americans were inferior and did not deserve the same rights as white Americans. Throughout the South, states passed "black codes." The laws varied from state to state, but in general they gave white citizens more power and took away rights from African-Americans. Under these laws, public schools were closed to African-Americans. Some laws prevented them from owning land, voting, or serving on juries. The codes restricted the jobs that African-Americans could hold, and often the jobs were as bad as the slavery they had endured. Some laws even allowed states to send unemployed African-Americans to jail.

As blacks and whites grew angrier with one another, riots broke out. In Memphis and New Orleans, hundreds of people were killed or hurt.

On May 2, 1866, a riot broke out between blacks and whites in Memphis, Tennessee.

The Ku Klux Klan terrorized African-Americans throughout the South.

In the meantime, a group called the Ku Klux Klan was created. The members wore white masks over their faces to hide their identities. This group burned African-American churches and homes, trying to frighten the former slaves and prevent them from voting and exercising other rights they had gained.

After Abraham Lincoln was killed in April 1865, Andrew Johnson became president. Johnson was in an awkward position because he needed to make peace among the states, but he was from the South. He had even owned slaves before the Emancipation Proclamation had been issued. Some believed he was perfect for the job because he was a Southerner who had sided with the Union. But others were not sure if his loyalties were right for a nation that needed to heal.

To make matters worse, a number of former Confederate leaders held political positions. The Northern leaders did not think this was fair. After other wars, leaders of the losing side were

President Andrew Johnson

often imprisoned. President Johnson and his government were allowing most of the former Confederate leaders to remain free, but many members of Congress did not feel they should be governors or other elected officials. Congress refused to accept these officials. As a result, after 1865 political offices became open to other Southerners, including African-Americans. They were also open to Northerners who moved to the South. These Northerners were called carpetbaggers, and their arrival would cause quite a stir in the South.

President Andrew Johnson speaks to onlookers from the back of a railroad car.

13

WHO WERE THE CARPETBAGGERS?

The term *carpetbaggers* was given to those people from the North who moved to the South after the Civil War. They were mostly former Union soldiers and members of the Republican Party, which had formed in the 1850s in order to oppose slavery. Southern members of the Democratic Party did not trust them. Southerners called these people carpetbaggers because they said the Northerners were able to pack all their "earthly belongings" in their bags. Many of these men carried carpetbags, which were suitcases made of carpetlike material.

Carpetbaggers came to the South for a number of reasons. Some were interested in politics. They wanted to run for office and gain power in the former Confederate states. Some were businessmen who saw opportunities to make money by starting new businesses during

14

*Southerners believed the carpetbaggers from the North
could carry all their belongings in carpetbags.*

Reconstruction. Other carpetbaggers included missionaries and teachers who wanted to help African-Americans gain an education and their civil rights.

There were groups of white Southerners who agreed with what the carpetbaggers were trying to do. They wanted to take part in the Reconstruction government. These Southerners were active in the Republican Party, and most did not support the Confederacy during the Civil War. The Southerners who did support the Confederacy called these people "scalawags" and considered them to be traitors.

A carpetbagger talks with a newly freed African-American.

16

THE EFFORTS OF THE CARPETBAGGERS

Many carpetbaggers had good intentions. They wanted Reconstruction to succeed, and they wanted to help the people of the South rebuild after the war. However, Reconstruction was a difficult time.

Congress tried to make Reconstruction work by passing both the 14th Amendment to the U.S. Constitution and the Reconstruction Act. Passed in June 1866 and ratified in 1868, the 14th Amendment protected the rights of African-Americans in the South. It also restricted the amount of power that former Confederate supporters could have. In March 1867, Congress passed the Reconstruction Act—even after President Johnson had vetoed it. The act required all former Confederate states to adopt a new state constitution—one that allowed all men, regardless of race, to vote. (Women did not have the right to vote until 1920.)

In 1867, Congress began talking about impeaching President Johnson. Many wanted to remove him from office, in part because they felt he wasn't leading the Reconstruction efforts as he should have.

Key (map legend):
- Military district 1
- Military district 2
- Military district 3
- Military district 4
- Military district 5
- Union states
- Confederate states

Map shows boundaries of 1867

CANADA

Maine
Rockland
Orwell · Vt.
N.H.
Portland
Littleton
New York
Mass.
West Brookfield
Conn.
Rhode Island
West Point
Lake Superior
Lake Huron
Lake Ontario
Lake Erie
Lake Michigan

Minnesota
Wisconsin
Michigan
Pennsylvania
New Jersey
Delaware
Washington, D.C.
Maryland

Dakota Territory

Nebraska Territory
Iowa
Illinois
Indiana
Ohio
West Virginia
Virginia

Colorado Territory
Kansas
McLeansboro
Missouri
Kentucky
North Carolina
South Carolina

New Mexico Territory
Indian Territory (Unorganized)
Arkansas
Tennessee
Memphis
Atlantic Ocean

Mississippi
Alabama
Georgia

Louisiana
Texas
New Orleans
Galveston
Florida

Gulf of Mexico

MEXICO

0   150   300 miles
0   150   300 kilometers

N / E / W / S

The Reconstruction Act divided the South into five military districts.

The Reconstruction Act protected the rights of Southern African-Americans, including their right to vote.

They believed his Reconstruction plan was too generous to the former Confederates. Johnson was almost removed from office, but he was spared impeachment by just one vote in the Senate.

Congress held an impeachment trial for President Johnson.
The president, however, was not present at the trial.

IN SERVICE TO THE SOUTH

As leaders worked on Reconstruction, some carpetbaggers were getting elected to political office in the South. More than 60 carpetbaggers were elected to Congress, and 10 served as governors. Among them was Harrison Reed. He was born in Littleton, Massachusetts, and worked for the Treasury Department in Washington, D.C. In 1863, President Lincoln sent Reed to Florida to be a tax commissioner. Two years later, President Johnson appointed him as postal agent for Florida.

Harrison Reed

Then, after the state's new constitution was adopted in 1868, he ran for governor of Florida and won.

Reed tried to help the state, but it was not easy. In that state, many members of the Republican Party were fighting among themselves. Reed had a hard time getting anything done. After his term was over, he spent time on his farm and worked as editor of the *Semi-Tropical*, a magazine about Southern agriculture.

Daniel Chamberlain was another carpetbagger who tried to make a difference. He was born in West Brookfield, Massachusetts, and served as an officer with the 5th Massachusetts Cavalry during the Civil War. In 1866, he moved to South Carolina. Two years later, he entered politics.

He worked as attorney general for the state and also served on the financial board. This agency was guilty of corruption, and Chamberlain criticized the group's dishonest actions.

Though he was a Republican, Chamberlain often sympathized with and supported the Southern Democrats. In 1874, he was elected governor of South Carolina. Once in office, he opposed the corrupt practices of his own political party and earned the support of many Democrats. However, all this changed when violence broke out in the state. In July 1876, some members of the African-American military were killed by a group of white Democrats.

Daniel Chamberlain

Chamberlain asked for federal troops to come to the state and keep peace. This angered the Democrats, who then refused to support Chamberlain again.

Government troops kept the peace between whites and African-American in the South.

When he ran for reelection that year, Chamberlain faced a Democrat named Wade Hampton III. The race for governor was mean-spirited, and the Democrats threatened the lives of Republicans and many African-American voters. The vote was so close that Rutherford B. Hayes, who had just been elected president, had to help decide the winner. Many historians believe that South Carolina made a deal to help elect Hayes as president in exchange for his support of Hampton and a promise to withdraw troops from the state. After Hampton was named governor, Chamberlain left South Carolina and went to work as a lawyer in New York.

Albion Winegar Tourgee was a carpetbagger who tried to

Albion Winegar Tourgee

25

improve the lives of African-Americans. Tourgee was born in Ohio and served in the Union Army before moving to North Carolina in 1865. He was a member of the Republican Party and was a superior court judge from 1868 to 1874. He tried to expose the hateful practices of the Ku Klux Klan and even wrote a letter to the *New York Tribune* about the group's actions.

[From the Independent Monitor, Tuscaloosa, Alabama, September 1, 1868.]
A PROSPECTIVE SCENE IN THE CITY OF OAKS, 4TH OF MARCH, 1869.

" Hang, curs, hang!   *
*   *   Their* complexion is perfect gallows. Stand fast, good
fate, to *their* hanging!   *   *   *   *   *   *   *   If they be not born to be hanged, our case is miserable.''
The above cut represents the fate in store for those great pests of Southern society—
the carpet-bagger and scalawag—if found in Dixie's land after the break of day on the
4th of March next.

*The Ku Klux Klan threatened carpetbaggers and scalawags
in this illustration from an Alabama newspaper.*

Throughout his career, Tourgee worked to secure civil rights for former slaves. Though he eventually left North Carolina, he is remembered for representing Homer Plessy in the 1896 Supreme Court case *Plessy v. Ferguson*. This case involved Plessy, a man who was part African-American, who was accused of illegally riding in a white railway car in Louisiana. Tourgee argued the case before the Supreme Court and stated that the 14th Amendment made such rules unfair.

The court ruled against Plessy and in favor of John Howard Ferguson, the Louisiana judge who originally found the man guilty. Of course, today we would see this case much differently and support the right of a person of any race to sit wherever he or she pleases. This was not the way things were in the late 1800s, though. Not until the civil rights movement of the 1950s and 1960s would African-Americans finally receive the rights they deserved.

Moses B. Walker

In Texas, one of the most successful carpetbaggers was Moses B. Walker. He was originally from Ohio and served in the Ohio Senate. During the Civil War, he fought for the Union and was colonel of the 31st Ohio Volunteer Infantry. After the war, Walker was part of a military unit that was sent to Texas. There he served as a judge and was later given a seat on the state Supreme Court. When a new governor was elected, Walker lost his seat on the court and then left the state. Though his time in Texas was short, Walker worked to help the state grow stronger during Reconstruction. He held the highest office in the Texas state government attained by any carpetbagger during Reconstruction.

28

George Thompson Ruby was another Texas carpetbagger. He was born a free African-American in New York and later lived in Portland, Maine. In 1864, he moved to Louisiana and worked as a schoolteacher there. He left Louisiana two years later after being beaten by an angry white mob as he tried to establish a school. Ruby moved to Galveston, Texas, and began working with the Freedmen's Bureau.

He also worked as a correspondent for the *New Orleans Tribune* and was a teacher at the Methodist Episcopal Church in Galveston. In 1869, he was elected to the state Senate in a mostly white district, and he later helped organize the first Labor Union of

George Thompson Ruby

Colored Men at Galveston. Some people believe that Ruby was the most influential African-American politician in Texas during Reconstruction.

30

State governments elected several African-Americans to political office during Reconstruction.

CARPETBAGGERS AND CORRUPTION

Not all carpetbaggers had the best interests of the South in mind. Although many came to the South to help its people rebuild, others came solely to gain wealth and power for themselves. A number of Northern businessmen took advantage of the South in order to make money. For example, some men in the lumber industry convinced Congress to sell them Southern forestland for a cheap price. One group bought 1 million acres for only 45 cents an acre.

Government corruption was a problem. State debt was high at the beginning of Reconstruction, and it got even worse with corrupt leaders in control.

Henry Clay Warmoth was a carpetbagger responsible for one of Louisiana's most corrupt administrations.

Henry Clay Warmoth

Warmoth was a lawyer originally from Mcleansboro, Illinois. After serving in the Union Army, he moved to Louisiana and convinced the newly freed slaves that he could help them. In 1868, at the young age of 26, he was elected governor of Louisiana. During his time in office, the state debt went from $6 million to $25 million. He made a lot of money by buying and selling state bonds, knowing that the state debt was rising.

In 1872, just 35 days before his term was over, Warmoth was impeached. He was not allowed to finish his last days in office.

As governor of Louisiana, William Pitt Kellogg faced impeachment charges as well. Kellogg was born in Orwell, Vermont, and served in the 7th Illinois Cavalry during the Civil

William Pitt Kellogg

War. After the war, he was appointed as collector of the
Port of New Orleans and soon after represented Louisiana
in the U.S. Senate. In 1873, he was elected governor of
Louisiana. While in office, he was accused of misusing
money and was impeached by the lower house of the state
Legislature. The charges were dismissed. After his term

*In 1874, Kellogg's government was overthrown by an angry mob, but Ulysses S. Grant,
who was president at the time, sent in federal troops to restore him to power.*

33

as governor ended, Kellogg returned to the U.S. Senate and served there for several more years.

Carpetbagger Adelbert Ames was born in Rockland, Maine, and graduated from the U.S. Military Academy at West Point. After serving as a general in the Union Army, he moved to Mississippi and was appointed governor. He also served Mississippi as a U.S. senator and later was elected governor. Like many carpetbaggers of the time, Ames was not personally corrupt, but he was not energetic or committed enough to Reconstruction to fight the corruption around him. Although he was a weak leader, Ames was one of the few carpetbaggers to call for economic security for African-Americans.

Adelbert Ames

THE FAILURE OF RECONSTRUCTION

Despite the carpetbaggers' efforts, honest and dishonest, Reconstruction was difficult and complicated. People tried to improve the Southern states by building new roads and schools, but taxes had to be raised to fund the projects. This angered many of the white Southerners who were still bitter about losing the Civil War.

A lot of people were also angry about the number of African-Americans who were holding political positions.

This portrait shows some of the first African-Americans elected to the U.S. Congress: from left, Hiram Revels, Benjamin Turner, Robert DeLarge, Josiah Walls, Jefferson Long, Joseph Rainy, and R. Brown Elliot.

35

Many white Southerners believed African-Americans should not even be free, let alone hold political office. They were not convinced that slavery was wrong. They did not like the fact that African-Americans had the right to own property and have good jobs.

President Ulysses S. Grant

After President Johnson left office, Ulysses S. Grant was elected president. Many Americans believed Grant would be able to put an end to the turmoil. He had been a hero of the Union Army and was loved by many Americans. However, Grant was ineffective as a political leader. Once in office, he seemed to be overwhelmed by the scope of the problem. Much of the government was corrupt while he was president, and Grant seemed unable to stop it.

In 1876, Rutherford B. Hayes was elected president, and Reconstruction for the most part came to a close. Fulfilling the promise that got him elected, Hayes pulled all of

President Rutherford B. Hayes

the federal troops out of the South. In doing so, he allowed some of the old Southern leaders to come to

Many poor African-Americans could not afford to pay the fee required to vote.

power again. These leaders passed a poll tax, which prevented many African-Americans from voting.

Although the Ku Klux Klan had largely been shut down by 1871, other groups had formed to frighten and harm African-Americans—and anyone who tried to help

38

them. Those who had really wanted to help the former slaves became discouraged and gave up. Before long, most of the carpetbaggers left the South and moved back to the North.

Some Southerners continued to harass African-American voters.

In this political cartoon, a woman who represents the South is crushed under the weight of a carpetbagger, who is protected by the military.

New practices called segregation were soon put into place in the South. African-Americans were not allowed to be in the same areas as white Americans. They had separate waiting rooms in train stations and doctors' offices. They had separate seating on buses and trains. They even had to use separate restrooms and water fountains.

Soon the former slaves found themselves without freedom once again. As the African-American writer W. E. B. DuBois explained, "The slave went free; stood a brief moment in the sun; then moved back toward slavery."

Some carpetbaggers had really tried to make a better South, while others were interested only in their own gain. But no matter their intentions, the efforts of the carpetbaggers were ultimately not enough. The failure of Reconstruction was a terrible blow to the rights of African-Americans. They would struggle for many more decades before the civil rights movement began and their fight for equality was finally addressed.

Although African-Americans had been freed from slavery, they did not yet have the civil rights enjoyed by white Americans.

41

GLOSSARY

civil rights—individual rights, of freedom and equal treatment, which all citizens have

corruption—dishonesty and deception, often involving illegal practices having to do with money

Democratic Party—one of the main political parties in the United States; after the Civil War, most Southerners were Democrats

Emancipation Proclamation—an act signed by President Abraham Lincoln in 1863 that freed all slaves

impeaching—bringing criminal charges against a public official

inaugurated—sworn into public office with a formal ceremony

poll tax—a fee charged to people before they could vote

ratified—officially approved

Republican Party—one of the main political parties in the United States; after the Civil War, most Northerners were Republicans

vetoed—refused to approve a legal act

DID YOU KNOW?

- When it was originally used, the term *carpetbagger* was a negative one. Today, the word just describes a politician who takes advantage of opportunity. When Hillary Rodham Clinton moved to New York to run for the U.S. Senate in 2000, many people called her a carpetbagger.

- Andrew Johnson's last important official act as U.S. president was a proclamation on Christmas Day 1868—a complete pardon of all Southerners who had taken part in the Civil War.

- By 1867, the Freedmen's Bureau had established 45 hospitals. By 1870, because of the organization's efforts, about 250,000 African-Americans were enrolled in schools.

- During Reconstruction, 45 carpetbaggers served in the U.S. House of Representatives, 17 served in the U.S. Senate, and 10 served as state governors.

IMPORTANT DATES

Timeline

1863	The Emancipation Proclamation is issued.
1865	The Freedmen's Bureau is created; the Civil War ends; President Lincoln is killed, and President Johnson takes office.
1866	The 14th Amendment is passed.
1867	The Reconstruction Act is passed, even though President Johnson vetoes it; impeachment proceedings begin against President Johnson but ultimately fail.
1868	The 14th Amendment is ratified.
1869	Andrew Johnson leaves office, and Ulysses S. Grant becomes president of the United States.
1877	Rutherford B. Hayes is inaugurated as president of the United States
1896	Racial discrimination is upheld in *Plessy v. Ferguson*.

IMPORTANT PEOPLE

ADELBERT AMES (1835-1933)
Carpetbagger who served as governor of Mississippi

DANIEL CHAMBERLAIN (1835-1907)
Carpetbagger who served as governor of South Carolina

WILLIAM PITT KELLOGG (1830-1918)
Carpetbagger who served as governor of Louisiana

HARRISON REED (1813-1899)
Carpetbagger who served as governor of Florida

GEORGE THOMPSON RUBY (1841-1882)
Carpetbagger who served in the Texas Senate

ALBION WINEGAR TOURGEE (1838-1905)
Attorney who represented Homer Plessy in Plessy v. Ferguson

MOSES B. WALKER (1819-1895)
Carpetbagger who served in the Supreme Court of Texas

HENRY CLAY WARMOTH (1842-1931)
Carpetbagger who served as governor of Louisiana

WANT TO KNOW MORE?

At the Library

Hakim, Joy. *Reconstructing America*. New York: Oxford University
    Press, 2002.

Heinrichs, Ann. *The Ku Klux Klan: A Hooded Brotherhood*. Chanhassen,
    Minn.: The Child's World, 2002.

Nardo, Don. *Andrew Johnson*. Danbury, Conn.: Children's Press, 2004.

Williams, Jean Kinney. *Ulysses S. Grant*. Minneapolis: Compass Point
    Books, 2002.

On the Web

For more information on *The Carpetbaggers,* use FactHound to
track down Web sites related to this book.

1. Go to *www.facthound.com*

2. Type in a search word related to this book
    or this book ID: 0756508347.

3. Click on the *Fetch It* button.

Your trusty FactHound will fetch the best Web sites for you!

On the Road

**Abraham Lincoln Home
National Historic Site**

413 S. Eighth St.

Springfield, IL 62701-1905

217/492-4241

To tour Lincoln's home and

learn more about his life

**Andrew Johnson
National Historic Site**

121 Monument Ave.

Greeneville, TN 37743

423/638-3551

To visit Johnson's two homes

and his grave

Look for more We the People books about this era:

The Assassination of Abraham Lincoln

The Battle of Gettysburg

The Emancipation Proclamation

The Underground Railroad

Great Women of the Civil War

A complete list of We the People titles is available on our Web site:
www.compasspointbooks.com

INDEX

About the Author

Lucia Raatma received her bachelor's degree in English literature from the University of South Carolina and her master's degree in cinema studies from New York University. She has written a wide range of books for young people. When she is not researching or writing, she enjoys going to movies, practicing yoga, and spending time with her family. She lives in New York.